How Much Money Is Enough?

While many people have opinions about how much money is enough for a Christian, I wonder just how many have searched the Scripture to see the amount of money God expects His children to have. I must confess that when I researched the financial requirements, I was astounded! I had to immediately admit that I didn't have enough money to do all the things God requires of me.

Let's look at twelve things God requires every believer to do. Notice that each of these things takes money.

I. God requires you to have enough money to *be truly joyful when you tithe.*

Tithing is not always joyful, especially when every cent counts and there are needs on every hand. In spite of their needs, there are many Christians who

T5-AFR-327

tithe faithfully. However, when money is in short supply, it's really hard to be joyful about it. Let's go to the Scripture and see what God says our attitude should be when we tithe.

Deuteronomy 26 is completely dedicated to the proper way of bringing the tithe to God. I recommend that you read the whole chapter at your earliest convenience. However, to save time, let's look at only a portion of it.

> And thou shalt *rejoice* in every good thing which the Lord thy God hath given unto thee, and unto thine house. . . .
>
> When thou hast made an end of tithing all the tithes of thine increase . . . .
>
> Deuteronomy 26:11,12

God says we must be in an attitude of rejoicing when we tithe. Think about it a moment. Just how much money will you have to earn to be really joyful each time you tithe? I cannot personally answer that question for you. You will have to determine that for yourself. There is an amount of money that would make tithing more than an act of obedience, turning it into a truly *joyful* act of worship.

But wait! Don't put the book down yet, for God requires you to have money for eleven other things.

II. God requires you to have enough money to *be able to adequately do your part to send the gospel of Jesus Christ throughout the whole world.*

I am sure all Christians know God requires more of them than just tithing. Malachi tells us we have robbed God if we do not give offerings over and above our tithes.

> **Will a man rob God? Yet ye have robbed me. But ye say, Wherein have we robbed thee? In tithes *and offerings.*
> Malachi 3:8**

Just take a moment and think of the many offerings God requires of you. Surely He wants you to give to missions, traveling ministers, as well as Christian radio and television networks.

Those who are taught the Word of God should help their teachers by paying them.
Galatians 6:6 TLB

Go . . . teach all nations, baptizing them in the name of the Father, and of the Son, and of the Holy Ghost:

Teaching them to observe all things whatsoever I have commanded you: and, lo, I am with you alway, even unto the end of the world. Amen.
Matthew 28:19, 20

Everyone knows that going into all the world to preach the gospel to every living soul is a very expensive business. However, this requirement becomes even more expensive when you fully understand what Jesus added to the Great Commission in the Book of Acts.

> . . . ye shall receive power, after that the Holy Ghost is come upon you: and ye shall be witnesses unto me *both* in Jerusalem, and in all Judea, and in Samaria, and unto the uttermost part of the earth.
>
> Acts 1:8

Notice carefully the word *both* in the above verse. It shows us how we are to witness in Jerusalem, Judea, Samaria, and the uttermost parts of the world. The word *both* as it is used here, means "simultaneously."

Let me paraphrase the verse to emphasize the vastness the word *both* adds to the Great Commission. "You shall be witnesses of me *simultaneously* in Jerusalem, and in Judea, and in Samaria, and unto the uttermost parts of the earth."

Now before you throw up your hands in utter hopelessness, let me point out that

5

God hasn't left you powerless and alone to meet this great expense. Look once again at the first part of the verse.

> . . . ye shall receive *power,* after that the Holy Ghost is come upon you . . . [then] ye shall be witnesses. . . .

> Acts 1:8

The power Jesus promises after the Holy Ghost comes upon you is *enabling power* (dunamis). The Greek word *dunamis* means "ability." So let's look at the verse again as I expand the paraphrase for you. "You shall receive *the ability* after the Holy Ghost has come upon you, and you will be able to witness of me simultaneously in Jerusalem, and in Judea, and in Samaria, and to the uttermost parts of the earth."

How much money will be enough for you to be able to joyfully tithe, as well as paying your fair share toward simultaneously sending the gospel of

Jesus Christ throughout the entire earth by every means God has ordained?

Now stay with me. We still have ten more things God says you must do that require money.

III. God requires you to have enough money to *contribute your fair share toward a better-than-average standard of living for your minister.*

Most churches simply ignore this requirement and take financial advantage of their ministers. Let me share a humorous saying about the prayer many churches offer when they hire a new preacher. "Lord, you keep our new preacher humble, and we, here at the church, will keep him poor."

Notice how different the above prayer is from God's instructions.

Let the elders that rule well be counted worthy of *double honor,*

especially they who labor in the word and doctrine.

For the scripture saith, Thou shalt not muzzle the ox that treadeth out the corn. And, *The laborer is worthy of his reward.*

1 Timothy 5:17,18

Notice it doesn't say your minister should receive just a living wage. Neither does it say he should receive an average wage. It clearly states that ministers of the gospel who handle the Word of God are worthy of *double honor.* That means *at least* twice as much money as the average wage-earner in your community.

There are good reasons God wants your minister to receive ample funding. First of all, your minister has the most important job in your nation. He watches for the souls of people, while civil authorities merely watch for their bodies and possessions.

Second, your man of God cannot lead you into the abundance you need to do all

8

God wants you to do if he, himself, is walking in insufficiency. It's difficult for your minister to take you where he has never been. Just as a lost pastor cannot produce a saved church, if your pastor walks in insufficiency, it will be difficult for him to bring you into the abundance you need to do all that God requires of you.

Just how much money will be enough for you to meet God's financial requirements for tithing with real joy, giving offerings large enough to do your fair share of preaching the gospel simultaneously to every corner of the globe, as well as giving your part for your minister to have a better-than-average income?

At this point we have covered three financial requirements, and we still have nine to go.

IV. God requires you to have enough money to *properly provide for those of your own house.*

Most people would not have made this requirement number four; they would have made it number one.

It took me a bit of time to find God's divine order in listing the twelve things God requires you to do that take money. I used two scriptures to help me make my decision.

> . . . seek ye first the kingdom of God, and his righteousness; and all these things shall be added unto you.
>
> **Matthew 6:33**

This verse tells us which of the several expenses of life should be first. Without question, it should be those that pertain to the Kingdom of God. Therefore, I placed the first three financial requirements as you find them. However,

Matthew 6:33 doesn't tell us what should be next.

Most people's responsibilities fall into three areas—*family, vocation,* and *God.* I found a scripture in the Old Testament that shows the divine order of these three parts of your life. In the following verse you will see the priority Isaac gave to these important aspects of his life after moving to Beersheba.

> . . . he *builded an altar* there, and called upon the name of the Lord, and *pitched his tent* there: and there Isaac's servants *digged a well.*
>
> **Genesis 26:25**

Isaac's first act was to build an altar, seeing to the things of God before anything else. Afterwards, he took care of his family by pitching his tent. Last of all, he took care of his vocation. His servants dug a well, for he was a well-digger by trade.

With this biblical model as a guide, we see that taking care of your family should be next.

> . . . if any provide not for his own, and specially for those of his own house, he hath denied the faith, and is worse than an infidel.
>
> **1 Timothy 5:8**

Everyone who has a family knows how expensive it is to raise children, especially if you hope to give them a proper education.

You must decide how much money will be enough for you to tithe joyfully, give acceptable offerings, provide adequately for your minister, as well as taking proper care of your family. If you will notice, these things are starting to add up to some real money, but wait. There's more!

V. God requires you to have enough money to *give good gifts to your children.*

How discouraging it must be to children of Christian families who must always hear that after tithing and giving to missions, there just isn't enough money for them to have any of their heart's desires. This type of disappointment can embitter children long after they become adults. Hear the Word of God on this matter.

> . . . **What man is there of you, whom if his son ask bread, will he give him a stone?**
>
> **Or if he ask a fish, will he give him a serpent?**
>
> *If ye then, being evil, know how to give good gifts unto your children,* **how much more shall your Father which is in heaven give good things . . . ?**
>
> Matthew 7:9-11

Please don't misunderstand. I am not encouraging you to spoil your children. Good parents have to teach their children the value of things. However, the Bible says never satisfying their heart's desire will eventually affect them.

> **Hope deferred maketh the heart sick. . . .**
>
> **Proverbs 13:12**

Think about it. Just how much money must you have to tithe with a joyful heart, properly fund the gospel outreach, give to amply support your minister, provide a good living and education for your family, as well as giving good gifts to your children?

I assume this is impacting you as much as it did me.

VI. God requires you to have enough money to *have a good savings account.*

Statistics tell us the average American has only **$2,365.91** in savings. I believe many of God's people have less. I came to this conclusion because of a startling statistic I found in the book, *31 Reasons People Do Not Receive Their*

Financial Harvest.[*] It stated that 40 percent of the bankruptcies in the United States involve born-again Christians. This statistic should be reason enough for every Christian to start saving money. However, there is an even better reason for saving. The Bible says God wants you to have enough money to be able to set aside a substantial amount.

Deuteronomy 28 contrasts the believer who does what God commands, with the one who refuses. I recommend you read it in the near future. For our study, I will deal with only a part of it.

. . . it shall come to pass, if thou shalt hearken diligently unto the voice of the Lord thy God, to observe and to do all his commandments . . . .

Blessed shall be thy basket and thy *store*.

Deuteronomy 28:1 & 5

*
Dr. Mike Murdock, Wisdom International, Inc., Dallas, TX 75221.

God blesses obedient Christians in their basket as well as in their store. *The store* speaks of that which you are setting aside, or storing up for a later date. From these verses we can see that God expects you to have financial reserves.

The list of blessings goes on for 14 verses in this chapter. Then in verse 15, God tells us what will happen to those who walk contrary to God's will. They will have no savings.

> **. . . it shall come to pass, if thou wilt not hearken unto the voice of the Lord thy God . . . that all these curses shall come upon thee, and overtake thee:**
>
> **Cursed shall be thy basket and thy *store.***
>
> **Deuteronomy 28:15 & 17**

It's obvious from these scriptures that God wants you to have a substantial amount of money in savings.

Please consider one more scripture that reinforces God's requirement of your having substantial savings.

A good man leaveth an inheritance to his children's children. . . .

Proverbs 13:22

God says a good person leaves an inheritance for his children, as well as his grandchildren.

This thing is getting serious! Just how much money will it take for you to joyfully tithe, give proper offerings to evangelize the world, do your part to provide for a better-than-average living for your minister, take proper care of your family, give good gifts to your children, as well as having a substantial savings account?

Hold on tight, for we are only half way through the list of twelve things God requires you to do that take money.

VII. God requires you to have enough money to *fund a proper retirement plan.*

Preparing for retirement is expensive business, especially when you take into account the process called "inflation." Here is a good illustration of how quickly the value of money deteriorates.

I entered the work force in the second half of the 1950s. At that time, $5,000 to $7,000 a year was a better-than-average income. A person could buy a nice home for about $12,000. New automobiles cost about $1,600. At that time, the military was offering a special retirement program. They promised $7,500 per year to anyone who would enlist for twenty years.

Now let's see how much this $7,500 annual retirement benefit was worth at the end of their enlistment. In the late 1970s, just twenty years later, a nice home was selling for about $75,000, and a new automobile cost around $5,000. As you can see, inflation had eaten away much of the money's value.

You must keep in mind that while you are setting aside money today for future retirement, the money you save will probably be worth only 20 percent of the value it has when you save it.

The next question you should be asking is, "Does the Bible say anything about retirement?"

> **Go to the ant, thou sluggard; consider her ways, and be wise:**
>
> **Which having no guide, overseer, or ruler,**
>
> *Provideth her meat in the summer, and gathereth her food in the harvest.*
>
> **Proverbs 6:6-8**

I won't attempt to tell you exactly how much to invest each month for your retirement. Only a qualified professional should help you answer that question. God merely wants me to make you aware of His requirement for you to gather and store enough finances while you are young to see you comfortably through old age.

Here we go again with the same haunting question. How much money will be enough for you to tithe joyfully, give your fair share to evangelizing the world, do your part to provide your pastor with a better-than-average income, take proper care of your family, provide good gifts for your children, and have a savings account, while also funding a proper retirement plan?

VIII. God requires you to have enough money to *pay all of your bills in a timely manner.*

No one should ever have to use the word "deadbeat" to describe a Christian. However, there is an ever-increasing number of Christians with the reputation of not paying their bills.

The Word of God says when you walk as God wants you to walk, you will have plenty of money available for day to day expenses, making it possible for you to pay all your bills in a timely manner.

And all these blessings shall come on thee, and overtake thee, if thou shalt hearken unto the voice of the Lord thy God.

Blessed shall be *thy basket* and thy store.

Deuteronomy 28:2 & 5

Here we see it again. Blessings, are supposed to overtake you in your *basket* (the money you use to meet your daily expenses).

Contrast this with the financial position of the disobedient child of God from verse 15 and beyond.

But it shall come to pass, if thou wilt *not* hearken unto the voice of the Lord thy God . . . all

these curses shall come upon thee, and overtake thee:

Cursed shall be thy basket **and thy store.**

Deuteronomy 28:15 & 17

There is no possible way for me to determine exactly how much money you will need to pay all your bills on time each and every month. That is something you will have to decide.

How much money will be enough for you to joyfully tithe, help evangelize the world, provide a good lifestyle for your minister, take proper care of your family, give good gifts to your children, have a substantial savings account, fund a proper retirement plan, and pay your bills on time every month?

IX. God requires you to have enough money to *pay your taxes.*

In Matthew 22, the legalists confronted Jesus. They tried to trap Him with this question, "Is it lawful to give tribute (pay taxes) to Caesar?"

Jesus knew it was a trick question, so He asked to see the coin used to pay the tax. When they showed it to Him, He inquired, "Whose picture is on the coin?"

They answered, "It's Caesar's picture."

Then Jesus replied:

> . . . Render therefore unto Caesar the things which are Caesar's. . . .
> Matthew 22:21

This verse answers everything we need to know about our obligation to pay taxes. Jesus says to pay them. However, it's up to you to decide how much money will be enough to pay your taxes, plus enough to tithe joyfully, help evangelize the world, provide a good lifestyle for your minister, take good care of your family, give gifts to your children, have a nice savings account, fund a proper retirement plan, while paying your bills on time.

X. God requires you to have enough money to *never have to borrow money to live.*

Two verses immediately come to mind when I think of borrowing money!

> No servant can serve two masters: for either he will hate the one, and love the other; or else he will hold to the one, and despise the other. Ye cannot serve God and mammon.

> **Luke 16:13**

Compare this verse to:

> . . . the borrower is servant to the lender.

> **Proverbs 22:7**

Your Bible says borrowing makes you a servant of the lender. The Bible also tells you that as a servant of the lender, you will not be able to properly serve God.

Now before you are overwhelmed by this statement, I must bring to your attention that God has a miracle solution to assist those who desire to be debt free. I will not attempt to teach you how to get out of debt in this booklet. However, I have written several books on the subject. I have also prepared "The Debt Free Army,"* a step-by-step program I designed to take believers out of debt.

In this booklet, I will give you just two of the many places in Scripture that teach miracle debt cancellation. See 2 Kings 4:1-7 where God miraculously canceled the debt of a widow and funded her retirement. Also see Nehemiah 5:1-12 where God miraculously took a whole nation out of debt in one day.

---

*   *For information on how to get out of debt, call 1-800-DEBT FREE.*

The Bible is clear. God expects you to have enough money to live debt free, tithe joyfully, help evangelize the world, provide a good lifestyle for your minister, take care of your family, give gifts to your children, have a proper savings account, fund your retirement plan, pay your bills on time, and keep your taxes up to date.

XI. God requires you to have enough money to *give generously to the poor.*

This responsibility will never end, for Jesus said the poor would always be among us.

> **For ye have the poor with you always. . . .**
>
> **Mark 14:7**

Not only will the poor always be among us, Jesus goes on to tell us He leaves it up to us how often we help them.

> **. . . *whensoever* ye will ye may do them good. . . .**
>
> **Mark 14:7**

Our Lord does not specify a percentage of your income that you should give to the poor. He simply says you are to help them as often as you will. It's totally up to you how much of your income you make available to the poor. With this information comes good news, as well as bad news.

First, the good news.

He that hath pity upon the poor lendeth unto the Lord; and that which he hath given will he pay him again.

Proverbs 19:17

In this verse we see two very important things about giving to the poor. First, a gift to the poor is actually a loan to God. Second, God promises to pay you back the money you give to the poor. Isn't it just like our Lord to put up His own good name for those who have no assets?

Now, the bad news.

**Whoso stoppeth his ears at the
cry of the poor, he also shall cry
himself, but shall not be heard.**

Proverbs 21:13

When you turn a deaf ear to the cry
of the poor, you automatically set a
negative force in motion. If you do not
assist the poor when they cry for help, you
will face a time when you will need help
in your own life. The Bible goes on to say
that when your time of need arises, no one
will hear your cry.

God wants you to have enough
money to give to every poor person who
asks something of you.

Once again, it's up to you to decide
how much money you will need to help
the poor people you meet during your
lifetime. Add this amount to the money it
will take for you to joyfully tithe, help
evangelize the world, provide a good
lifestyle for your minister, take good care
of your family, give nice gifts to your
children, have a substantial savings

account, fund a proper retirement plan, pay your bills on time every month, keep your taxes up to date, as well as never having to borrow.

XII. God requires you to have enough money to *lend to every believer who asks.*

This financial requirement is probably the biggest one Jesus ever gave His children. After twenty years of walking in the benefits of seedtime and harvest, I thought I might be arriving at a point where I had enough money to do everything God required of me. However, after realizing the magnitude of this requirement, I have had to start sowing more than ever before, for it has become obvious to me that I need much more money than I have.

Let me share two verses that staggered me. I hope they will be as important to you as they are to me.

> . . . him that would borrow of
> thee turn not thou away.
>
> Matthew 5:42

Jesus plainly says His children should have enough money to lend to everyone who asks. Add to this requirement the following instructions:

> If there be among you a poor man of one of thy brethren within any of thy gates in thy land which the Lord thy God giveth thee, thou shalt not harden thine heart, nor shut thine hand from thy poor brother:
>
> But thou shalt open thine hand wide unto him, and shalt surely lend him sufficient for his need, in that which he wanteth.
>
> For the poor shall never cease out of the land: therefore I command thee, saying, Thou shalt *open thine hand wide* unto thy brother, to thy poor, and to thy needy, in thy land.
>
> Deuteronomy 15:7,8 & 11

When you consider these divine directives, it becomes extremely difficult to determine exactly how much money you will actually need to properly pay for the twelve financial requirements God gives to every believer.

Why I Wrote This Booklet

I did not write this book to explain how to obtain the money it takes to meet all the financial requirements God places on His children. However, I feel I must say a few words to help dispel the hopeless feeling the preceding information might bring upon you. I have chosen just a few verses of Scripture that hold out God's promise of delivering more than enough money into your hands to do everything He requires of you.

> **According as his divine power hath given unto us all things that pertain unto life and godliness, through the knowledge of him. . . .**
> **2 Peter 1:3**

Carefully read this verse, for it tells you God's divine power is able to give you all things that are necessary for life and godliness. Notice that every one of the twelve things God requires us to have money for, falls into one of these two categories, either *life* or *godliness.*

Now unto him that is able to do exceeding abundantly above all that we ask or think. . . .
Ephesians 3:20

This verse goes even further by telling you God is able to do exceedingly abundantly above all you will be able to ask or even think. That means no matter how great the financial obligation God places upon you, even if it goes beyond your ability to imagine, your God has a plan for accomplishing it.

He that spared not his own Son, but delivered him up for us all, how shall he not with him also freely give us *all* things?
Romans 8:32

Just think about it, and you will see that nothing would be too much for God to give you, for He has already given you the most valuable thing in the universe. He gave His only begotten Son, Jesus, to save your soul. How could He ever deny you any other thing you would need to accomplish His will for your life?

Conclusion

It now becomes evident that God meant for His children to have much more money than even the most outspoken advocates of biblical economics and the life of abundance have been teaching. It is as the psalmist said.

> **Let them shout for joy, and be glad, that favor my righteous cause: yea, let them say *continually*, Let the Lord be magnified, which hath pleasure in the prosperity of his servant.**
> **Psalm 35:27**

Notice the psalmist tells us we must *continually,* not occasionally, but continually say, ". . . **Let the Lord be magnified, which hath pleasure in the prosperity of his servant.**" It is for this reason the writer of Proverbs says, "**The blessing of the Lord, it maketh rich, and he addeth no sorrow with it**" (Proverbs 10:22).

Add to this verse the fact that you are the seed of Abraham.

> . . . **if ye be Christ's, then are ye Abraham's seed, and heirs according to the promise.**
> **Galatians 3:29**

Notice, not only are you the seed of Abraham, but you are also the rightful heir of his promises. Notice further what these promises are.

> **Now the Lord had said unto Abram, Get thee out of thy country, and from thy kindred,**

and from thy father's house, unto a land that I will show thee:

And I will make of thee a great nation, and I will bless thee, and make thy name great; and thou shalt be a blessing:

And I will bless them that bless thee, and curse him that curseth thee: and in thee shall all families of the earth be blessed.

Genesis 12:1-3

This promise is staggering. Just think about it. How in the world will you ever obtain enough money to bless every family in the whole world? This covenant seems impossible, until you read about God's promise to supply.

. . . thou shalt remember the Lord thy God: for it is he that giveth thee power to get wealth, that he may establish his covenant which he sware unto thy fathers, as it is this day.

Deuteronomy 8:18

God Himself has given you supernatural power to get the wealth you will need to fulfill the covenant He has made with you on behalf of a lost and dying world.

Acknowledgment

This book is unlike any book I have previously written. It's different in its inception, for I received the inspiration to write it while reading the book, *31 Reasons People Do Not Receive Their Financial Harvest* by Dr. Mike Murdock, P.O. Box 99, Dallas, TX 75221.

While all of Dr. Murdock's books have blessed me, I believe this one is his best to date.

Thank you, Dr. Mike, for the influence your teachings have had on the lives of so many of God's children, and special thanks for the influence they have had on my life.

Copyright © 1998 by International Faith Center, Inc. P.O. Box 917001, Ft. Worth, TX 76117-9001. Printed in the United States of America. All rights reserved under International Copyright Law. Contents and/or cover may not be reproduced in whole or in part in any form without the express written consent of the publisher.

How Much Money Is Enough?
ISBN: 1-878605-27-5

Unless otherwise indicated, all Scripture quotations are taken from the *King James Version* of the Bible.
Verses marked **TLB** are taken from *The Living Bible*. Copyright © 1971. Used by permission of Tyndale House Publishers, Inc., Wheaton, Illinois 60189. All rights reserved.

HIS Publishing Company
P.O. Box 917001
Ft. Worth, TX 76117-9001

Order Form

Qty	Item	Title	Cost	Total
	1001	Always Abounding	6.95	
	1033	Breakthrough Prayer	5.95	
	1036	Debt-Free Guarantee	5.95	
	1007	Faith Extenders	8.95	
	1032	Financial Excellence	9.95	
	1009	Hundredfold	8.95	
	1027	It's Not Working	9.95	
	1028	John Answers	6.95	
	1038	Manifest Abundance	5.95	
	1012	Powerful Principles	7.95	
	1014	Stolen Property	5.95	
	1037	Better Than Money	5.95	
	1016	Wealth of World	7.95	
	1003	War On Debt	7.95	
	1013	Debt-Reduction	12.95	
	1022	The Victory Book	14.95	
	1023	Have Good Report	8.95	
	3046	Library of Above	79.95	
	3034	Debt Free Army	125.00	
		Subtotal		
		Shipping/Handling		
		Tax Deductible Donation		
		Total Enclosed		

Please make all purchases with U.S. funds.

Shipping/Handling Chart		
	U.S.	**Foreign**
Up to $10.00	1.50	3.00
$10.01 to $50.00	3.00	6.00
$50.01 to $100.00	5.00	10.00
$100.01 and up	Add 5%	Add 10%

( ) Enclosed is my check or money order made payable to **HIS Publishing Company.**

Please charge my: ( ) Visa ( ) MasterCard ( ) Discover ( ) American Express

Account # _____

Expiration Date_____

_____
Signature

To assure prompt and accurate delivery of your order, please take time to print all information neatly.

_____
Name

_____
Address

_____
City, State, & Zip Code

Phone: 1-800-521-5744
E-mail: savanzini@hispublishing.com
Mail: HIS Publishing Company
P.O. Box 917001
Ft. Worth, TX 76117-9001